Journey To Joseon

Monarchs & Nobles (Tales From The Past)

Gigi Balita

Ukiyoto Publishing

All global publishing rights are held by

Ukiyoto Publishing

Published in 2022

Content Copyright © Gigi Balita

ISBN 9789360167769

All rights reserved.

No part of this publication may be reproduced, transmitted, or stored in a retrieval system, in any form by any means, electronic, mechanical, photocopying, recording or otherwise, without the prior permission of the publisher.

The moral rights of the author have been asserted.

This is a work of fiction. Names, characters, businesses, places, events, locales, and incidents are either the products of the author's imagination or used in a fictitious manner. Any resemblance to actual persons, living or dead, or actual events is purely coincidental.

This book is sold subject to the condition that it shall not by way of trade or otherwise, be lent, resold, hired out or otherwise circulated, without the publisher's prior consent, in any form of binding or cover other than that in which it is published.

All images/fanarts used inside the book are reproduced copy lifted from Google.

Biography of characters from Wikipedia.

Acknowledgement

I would like to acknowledge Ukiyoto Publishing for giving me this much coveted opportunity that every writer dreams, to be published in an international book. It is with much gratitude that I was given such a blessed chance to be able to share my talent to Indian readers whom I know to be people of deep thinking and comprehension. Such a joyous moment as I ponder and write this book. My immense gratitude and thankfulness dear Ukiyoto Publishing team.

I would also like to recognize and give credit to the artist of the painting I used in this book, my sister Owie Balita. It has been my personal conviction to use her art in all of my book covers. I don`t exactly know if it can be called divine intervention or simply coincidence, but every time I have a book for publication, it always corresponds to the fact that she has a new commissioned painting. I am also grateful to her friend Ms. Connie Reyes, who is the owner of the painting "The Garden of Morning Calm", for allowing me to use the said painting in the front cover of my book.

I would also like to acknowledge my family Owie, Edwin, Mich, Gab and Elize. Special mention to my uncle Resty Sugatan and cousin Lulu Sugatan for the moral support.

Foreword

This book **Monarchs & Nobles (Tales From The Past)** was divided into volumes from Korean dynasties to British monarchies to Indian nobilities and historical personalities who helped shape the world. It is my way of sharing with readers my love for the classics, and how those periods inspired me to write with such fascination about all times past.

Titled **Journey To Joseon**, this first volume is specifically about Korean dynasties, particularly about Joseon era. I started to watch the so-called KDramas and KoreaNovelas way back three years ago, after my resignation from my previous job. I may not be part of this Millennial generation that has become glued and grappled to their electronic media or screen monitor watching Korean telenovelas and KDramas. I may not have become an instant fan of K-pop, but Korean stories of the old equally interest me as much as other millenials enjoy a marathon of KGayo or Kmovie festivals from Rakuten Viki, Kocowa, Tubi, HLKA-TV and KBS. I must admit I am fascinated watching the likes of Empress Ki or Mr. Queen sort of stories. However, I must admit I am more of a reader, who obviously prefer to read books.

This book is my way of sharing that same fascination and captivation upon these stories, by presenting them to you in my most eloquent form of expression, through poetry. To all of you old souls like me, who derives pleasure in reading about old stuff, stories of long ago, lives lived in long times past, this book is for you.

Afterword

As we journeyed through time and travelled back and tried to reminisce the colourful history of Korea during its early reign, it can be aptly said Korea as a country today has successfully emerged into a niche of its own in the world, positioning itself as one of the world`s most developed country, not only in terms of economy and infrastructure development, but also in the field of Arts and Literature.

Presently, Korea`s literary genre catapulted into fame through the emergence of highly popular Koreanovelas and KDramas. With the emergence of KPop and famous Korean stars, Korean literature have come a long way, through the means of multimedia in the form of movies and Koreanovelas. This is the future of their art, the glory days of mainstream medium.

In the old standard, students study literature through books, in the confinement of their classrooms.Today, however, the young generation, including students, can learn Korea`s history through movies. On a different note, this is the author`s way of imparting and propagating not their industry, but their literary legacy through using the old school way, by writing their history through lyrical interpretation and story-telling.

This book is the author`s depiction of one of the most loved era in Korea`s history, the Joseon Dynasty. The author consider it a tremendous privilege to have written such an interesting part of history through this book, and highly recommend this book for students or people who would like to delve deeper in a more understanding aspect of Korea as a nation.

Contents

Introduction

Have you ever thought how it would be if you were born yesterday, at the time of monarchs and nobles, when people's ordinary wardrobe consists of extra ordinary materials and fabulous frills? When OOTDs (Outfit Of The Day) was not the trend, yet men and women of their time dress up conventionally in quite elegant fashion? Have you ever wished you were born same time, met a certain person, lived a life as exciting, as fascinating, as surreal as things seemed to be then?

No need to penetrate a parallel world, nor travel a portal and reach a time-bending existence. Or hurtle into the future, move into a spur of the past and grapple in the theory of general relativity. Or intersect with the alternate universe, multiverse and timeline, use the GPS (Global Positioning System) satellites wherein you reach a particular dimension.

Armed with enormous imagination, I try to reach a fancy world that once existed in reality, yet can simply be reminisce today. The long forgotten past that used to be the day to day existence of yesteryears will be brought to the present as we once again recall what was life back then, through a recollection of fragments and sliver of their past through my poems.

As I scan the pages of this book, and as I start to flip each page, allow me to bring you in a momentous time travel and sweep you back from the glorious past to travel down memory lane and once again let us reminisce the golden glory of kingdoms and palaces that used to grace our youthful imaginations and fantasies.

Joseon Dynasty

Joseon Dynasty or 'Great Chosun Country' was a Korean dynastic kingdom that lasted for approximately five centuries. It was the last dynasty of Korea and its longest-ruling Confucian dynasty, founded by Yi Seong-gye in July 1392 and replaced by the Korean Empire in October 1897. The history of Joseon is largely divided into two parts: the early period and the late period; some divide it into three parts, including a middle period.

Gyeongbuk Palace Throne Room Building

Crown Prince Hyomyeong

Born Yi Yeong, or Lee Yeong, and posthumously called King Munjo, was a prince of the Joseon Dynasty. The prince was the eldest son of King Sunjo, husband of Queen Sinjeong and father of King Heonjong. In 1819, he was titled Crown Prince of Joseon. A genius in literature and the arts, he created several court dances and used court ritual and the arts to validate and augment the King's control over the government. Known to have pursued various political reforms, the prince served as Regent in 1827 until his death 3 years later at age 20. He did have some enemies amongst his maternal relatives, but avoided nepotism and was a talented writer, composer and choreographer.

Moon Embracing The Sun

(Haereul pum eun Dal)

the moon embraced the sun

i saw the yellow tinge

shadowed by the silvery moon upon

i have felt as if the sun

melted under my gaze

that was how it was

the first time i ever saw your face.

the moon clasped the florid orange sun

and if it truly, had hands

wide and broad, as one

the sun would find itself

held in the deepest clutch

ever could be given

in its heliacal closeness that matched.

the moon enfolded the sun

as if it were not two spirits, but one

as if it owned the identity

of the golden sanguine deity

as if it possessed all the warmth and tenderness
emanating from its sweet emotion
and i heard the thumping sound of my heartbeat
beating with yours alone.

the moon cuddled the sun
and in their tight togetherness
they both danced to the beat of their own
nuzzled each body that even the spirit
transgress alone
the sun never for a moment forgets
the love and passion it has given with no regrets.

the moon hugged the sun
until they become one in unison
but then, suddenly
with bleakness and sad melancholy
the moon deserted its home
the sun became alone
with such a stirring loneliness
and emptiness that cannot be assuaged
by any cheerful smile of a child
nor of cheerful mirth brought by the rain

when death temporarily came
separation brought them pain.

the moon was detached from the sun
by sinful wicked notions and treachery
by vile jealous schemes and disharmony
another woman played the beldame well
and used a human talisman in a spell
they planted one vicious amoral ploy
together with a shaman to destroy
the beauty between two bosom buddies
who found its destiny
in each other`s eternal bind and connectivity.

the moon caressed the scorching sun
its life itself the strength, the force, the power
momentarily lose its way and gone
the shadows above went so much higher
the moon met its fate with the red sun
that moment i have come to know
our destiny has begun
my heart itself is not mine,
but only live to the glory

of your love and faithful devotion.
you and i are now together
after the moon travelled
in the land of the unknown
it defied the sense of mortality
and risen on its own
love is powerful than death
the soul resurrects from its previous hollow
to reunite and kindle its spirit once more to know
and feel a love through eternity
with its twinflame, its better half, its partner
its one and only significant other.

the lively effervescent moon
Queen Yoon
reunited with King Lee-Hwon
the faithful, loyal, trusting sun
and they live happily since together
the moment the moon embraced the sun
ever after.

"Rarely it comes in one`s life an extra ordinary kind of love that transcends time and dimension, defies death and afterlife. A love story like this is one in a million, as if written in the stars and sketched in the deepest of the ocean. The thread of Fate may have parted lovers apart, yet it is Destiny itself that leads a way for a long awaited reunion that will bind two hearts in the end."

Taejo Of Joseon

Born Yi Seong-gye, he was the founder and first ruler of the Joseon dynasty of Korea. After ascending to the throne, he changed his name to YiDan and reigned from 1392 to 1398. He was the main figure in the overthrowing of the Goryeo dynasty. Taejo abdicated in 1398 during a strife between his sons and died in 1408.

Taejo's father, Yi Ja-chun, was an official of Korean ethnicity serving the Mongol-led Yuan dynasty. Taejo's mother, Lady Choe, was a Goryeo woman from a prominent family originally from Deungju in present-day North Korea. Her father was a Korean chiliarch under the Yuan dynasty who commanded a mingghan.

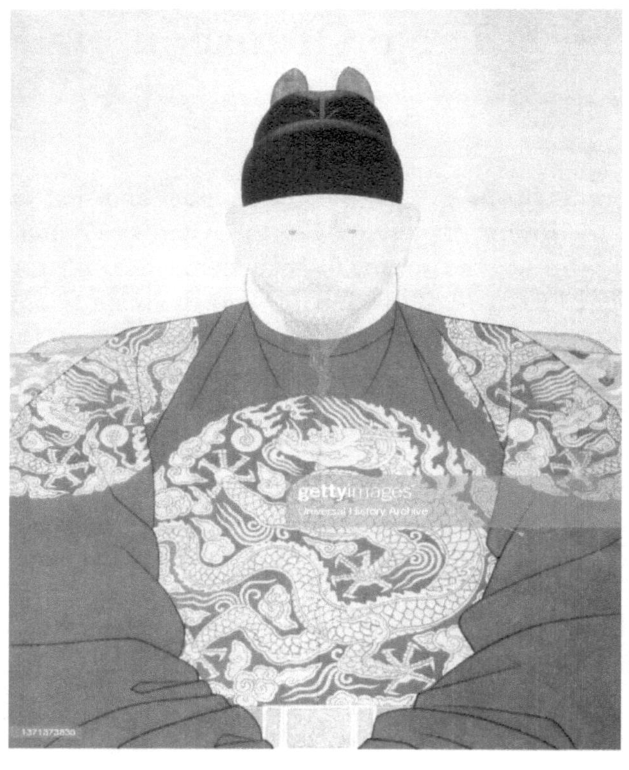

*Photo by: Universal History Archive/Universal Images Group
via Getty Images*

The Sons Of Taejo

King Taejo had two wives, the first one who gave
birth to six descendants

And his second wife, who had two sons from him,
perchance

The King favored his youngest son from his second
wife, his favorite

And backed him as the successor to his much coveted
seat.

King Taejo's fifth son from his first wife, Yi Bang-
won

Who later became King Taejong of Joseon

Led a coup along with many military officers

And brazenly killed his two younger half-brothers.

Prime Minister Jeong, and many of his faction

Yi Bang-won first tried to show that he was not
intended to take the throne

So he gave a push to his older brother Jeongjong to
be a crown prince

Although he dreamt also of the coveted crown
eversince

King Taejo was upset and then abdicated in disgust

And Jeongjong became king in the following year at
last

The same year he moved the capital back to
Gaegyeong, the old Goryeo capital

So a conflict broke out between Bang-won and his
older brother Bang-gan.

Bang-won's troop attacked and defeated that of Bang-
gan's army

He was an able, wise administrator though his reign
was bloody

He banned all kinds of private force on the advice of
Crown Prince Bang-won

He died in fourteen nineteen, and was buried
near Kaesong.

"The desire of power is a dangerous notion. Most people cannot handle it well. As a result, they allow power to overwhelm them instead of them controlling power in their hands. That is human error and folly. Power is a matter of perception. If you allow a certain power as a tool to use your authority over people, it will enter your head and give you a wrong notion and perspective about it. This kind of power can lead to blindness. Remember, power is like a two-way string, hold an easier grip. Don`t pull too much, don`t push in extreme either."

Jeongjong Of Joseon

Born Yi Bang-gwa, whose changed name is Yi Gyeong, was the second ruler of the Joseon Dynasty of Korea. He was the second son of King Taejo, the founder and first monarch of the dynasty.

Born in 1357 as Yi Bang-gwa, he was a prudent, generous, brave, and able military officer. During the latter days of the declining Goryeo Dynasty, Jeongjong followed his father, Yi Seong-gye, to various battlefronts and fought at his side. When his father became king in 1392, he became prince.

King Jeongjong, Getty Images, Universal History Archive

Jeongjong

Yi Bang-gwa, also known as Jeongjong later on in
history

Was a prudent, generous, brave, and able officer in
military.

During the latter days of the declining Goryeo
Dynasty

He followed his father to various battlefronts and
fought at his side bravely.

He became prince automatically anew

When his father became king in 1392.

Yi Bang-won first tried to show that he was not
intended to take the throne since

So he gave a push to his older brother Jeongjong to
be a crown prince.

However, he abdicated months later

And sat on his throne at the expense of his dear
brother.

The same year he moved the capital back to
Gaegyeong, the old Goryeo capital

Then a conflict broke out between Yi Bang-won and
his older brother, Yi Bang-gan.

King Taejo was upset and abdicated in disgust

And Jeongjong became king in the following year at
last.

Yi Bang-won's force attacked and defeated that of
Bang-gan's army

Bang-gan was then sent into exile along with his
family.

General Bak Bo, who persuaded Bang-gan to fight
against Bangwon, was executed

King Jeongjong, knowing that he was a mere political
figurehead.

He was an able, wise administrator even though his
short reign

Was marked by bloodshed within the royal family
then.

He banned all kinds of private troops on the advice of
Crown Prince Bang-won

He died in fourteen nineteen, and was buried
near Kaesong.

Queen Jeinwondeok

The wife and queen consort of Yi Yung, King Yeonsan, the 10th Joseon monarch. She was queen consort of Joseon from 1494 until her husband's deposition in 1506, after which she was known as Deposed Queen Sin. She didn't receive posthumous name as a queen after her death.

Lady Sin was born into the Geochang Sin clan on 15 December 1476 to Sin Seung-seon and Princess Jungmo. Her mother is the daughter of King Sejong's fourth son, Grand Prince Imyeong, and Prince Gwiseong, who served as Yeonguijeong during the reign of King Sejo, is the uncle of Lady Sin.

Queen Seondeok

The Temporary Queen

The tragic story of Yeok and Chae Kyung was a sad
ending

When the Queen was dethroned one week after her
crowning

The young girl was sent away from her wealthy family

She married the King at a young age, it was her
destiny.

Her parents were warned on her daughter`s fate by
prophecy

The prophesy which foretold her family`s misfortune
and adversity

Fate constantly throws the King and Chae Kyung
together

And it seemed that tragedy followed them at every
turn after.

It was a young girl`s tragic doom at only thirteen

She was cruelly called by the nation as their Deposed
Queen Shin

It was not an opulent and elegant life, far from the
fairy tale story

That`s supposed to be enjoyed by somebody of noble
royalty.

King Jungjong, also called Yi Yeok, the eleventh ruler
of Dynasty Joseon

Has succeeded to the throne after his half-brother`s
deposition

During his early reign, he could not exert regal
authority freely

For those who put him on the throne exercised
power immensely.

When the three main leaders of coup died of natural
causes and old age reason

Jungjong began to assert his authority and carried out
a government reformation

Jo Gwang-jo, his scholar, strengthened local
autonomy by establishing a self-governing rule

And promoted Confucian writings by translating
them into Korean hangul.

Jo believed that any talented people should be
appointed as officer

He enforced the laws strictly so that no one dared to
receive a bribe ever

After years of reformist agenda, Jungjong abandoned
Jo`s programs however

And executed him on charge of factionalism and
exiled his followers.

Jungjong`s reign was marked by tumultuous struggle
among various factions

Sometimes he was seen as a tragic figure who never
wanted to be a king to his nation

He deposed his loving queen under the pressure of
the coup leaders

His Queen Dangyeong, known as the Deposed
Queen Shin to others.

In the early days of reform, Jungjong encouraged
many books to be published

He also tried to improve self-government of local
areas, then accomplished

And succeeded in reforming the civil service
examination

He knew the importance of defense and encouraged
military service implementation.

After being Queen for seven days, Shin was expelled from the palace

In King Myeongjong's 12th year of reign, she died without any fuss

The King held a portrait of Lady Shin at the funeral ceremony

The Queen was buried in a family tomb according to the wishes of her family.

"Destiny might be inevitable. We may have been born with a pre destined fate. But all of us were given the gift of free will. And the power to choose what path of life to tread lies ultimately in our selves. Stars and the constellations` position might influence our lives in general, but they have nothing to do with our own thinking and decision. We humans are made to be the supreme creations who must be the pilots to navigate our own ships in order to arrive at our deserved destinations."

Queen Seondeok Of Silla

Reigned as Queen Regnant of Silla, one of the Three Kingdoms of Korea from 632 to 647.She was Silla's twenty-seventh ruler and its first reigning queen. She was the second female sovereign in recorded East Asian history and encouraged a renaissance in thought, literature, and the arts in Silla. In Samguksagi, Queen Seondeok was described as "generous, benevolent, wise, and smart". According to the Legend of Jigwi, she was even beautiful.

In January 632, Queen Seondeok became the first queen regnant of Silla. As a ruler, Queen Seondeok's primary concern was the livelihood of her people. Right after she was crowned, she appeased her people by telling them what her policies would be. She sent royal inspectors throughout the kingdom to improve the care of widows, widowers, orphans, the poor, and the elderly. During that same year, she sent a diplomat to pay tribute to the Emperor of the Tang dynasty of China, and inform him about Silla's new ruler. However, Emperor Taizong of Tang refused to acknowledge Seondeok as a ruler because she was a woman.

Queen Seondeok of Silla

Queen Seon Of Silla

SeonDeok, Silla's twenty-seventh ruler, and its first reigning queen in Silla

Born Princess Deokman, reigned as Queen Regnant of Korea

She was described as generous, benevolent, wise, and smart

She encouraged a renaissance in thought, literature, and the arts.

The thought of having a female ruler sitting on the throne was still unacceptable

So Princess Deokman had to prove herself to gain the trust and support of her people

Eventually, she succeeded, and was named as King Jinpyeong's successor

But some officials planned an uprising in order to stop her from being crowned thereafter.

Enemies planned a rebellion, but their plan was discovered and suppressed immediately

As punishment, Chilsuk was beheaded in the market place along with his entire family

Seokpum was able to escape but decided to return, exchanging clothes with a woodcutter

Upon his return, he was arrested by soldiers and was executed later.

Queen Seondeok's concern was the livelihood of her people primarily

After she was crowned, she appeased them by telling them what her policies would be

She sent royal inspectors throughout the kingdom to improve the care of everybody

Specially their widows, widowers, orphans, the poor and the elderly.

She sent a diplomat to pay tribute to Emperor Taizong of Tang in China

To inform him about the new ruler in the Kingdom of Silla

However, Taizong refused to acknowledge her as a ruler since she was a woman

So her attempt became futile, fruitless and barren.

In the second year of the Queen`s reign, she built the Star-Gazing Tower

An astronomical observatory to help the peasants and
farmers

Through this act of kindness, the queen won the
people's support and loyalty

And her position was strengthened against the
opposition of the male aristocracy.

It was an offering to the Buddha, in hope that these
wishes would be fulfilled

The Queen often visited the temple, to pray for
wisdom and her nation be healed

The tower still stands in the old Silla capital of
Gyeongju in old Silla

In South Korea and is the oldest surviving
observatory in East Asia.

In the same year, Queen Seondeok sent a diplomat
again

To pay tribute to the Tang Emperor for the second
time but then

Emperor Taizong refused to acknowledge her as a
ruler still

Eventually, no amount of prayers and medicine
worked when she became ill.

Strange things started to happen after the Queen`s
deteriorating condition

It was as though the Kingdom was coming into an
impending ominous situation

One day, a large stone on the south side of the
mountain moved on its own

Goguryeo attacked the mountain valley after several
months passed on.

The next year, the sea water on the eastern part of
Silla turned red

Which caused all of the fish living in it to perish to
succumb and dead

These events made the people anxious, and some of
them considered it all

As bad omens portending the Silla kingdom's
destruction and downfall.

Until Baekje and Goguryeo conquered Danghang
bastion

Blocking an important sea route to the Tang
dynasty`s succession

For the third time, the Queen sent a diplomat to
Emperor Tang

And asked for assistance, so the Emperor gave her
three proposals.

First, he would attack the Liaodong and carry out a
naval campaign

On the west in order to occupy the Baekje`s domain

Second, the emperor would provide thousands of
Tang uniforms and groups

Of army flags in order to help Silla soldiers disguise
themselves as Chinese troops.

Third, send a male royal of Tang to serve as a new
king of Silla,

Since Silla faced constant threat due to having a
female ruler Shin Ha

The diplomat returned to Silla, unable to tell the
Queen Seon

Of the proposals that the Tang Emperor have
presented and introduced on.

At that point of crisis, the Queen sent for the well
known Buddhist monk Jajang

Who had been studying under the great Buddhist
masters of the Dynasty Tang

He advised the queen and her counsels to build the
great nine-story pagoda

For the dual purpose of blocking foreign invasions
and calming the people of Silla.

After careful consideration, the queen decided to
accept Jajang's proposal

Seeing it as necessary to overcome the crisis they were
facing as usual

Her royal subjects were against it due to concern for
the state of the royal treasury

Since the construction of the pagoda will bring a
heavy tax burden on her people`s money.

Still the queen decided to continue with the plan with
such firm belief

That a work of religious devotion would bring her
people a solution and relief

The pagoda was finally completed and it was
called the Imperial Dragon Temple

And was considered the tallest in East Asia, towering
above others all.

Queen Seon also appointed a nobleman
named Bidam to the highest position

To unify the three Kingdoms under Silla was laid in
the first foundation

She faced her greatest challenge when some of her
highest officials started a rebellion

Bidam had a strong political influence in the court
and powerful dominion.

When the Queen`s health had deteriorated sharply
due to illness

And a star fell near the Queen's residence, it was
visualized as the way the ball bounces

Bidam, who saw the star, claimed it was a sign of the
queen's impending downfall

To encourage his superstitious followers and believers
all.

The queen, who heard of the event, became anxious
and fearful

But Kim Yushin calmed her by telling her not to
worry and be dreadful

For he himself had a plan together with Kim Alcheon

To eventually suppress the uprising of the rebellion.

He then flew a huge kite with a
burning scarecrow attached to it

To make it appear that the star was back in its place
and so fit

Bidam's followers saw this, and became discouraged
by such disappointment

Until they were executed and failed to overthrow the
government.

Like her father, Queen Seondeok was drawn to Buddhism as then

Silla built many temples, pagodas, and Buddha statues during her reign

The pagoda represented the earnest wish of the Queen and the Silla people together

To protect the country and bring the three kingdoms of Korea under one ruler.

"Sometimes the strength of a person doesn`t come from his character, but from other people`s weaknesses. His knowledge of his fellow`s disadvantages fuels him to find his own inner strength".

Large and charming peonies have long been called the "king of flowers" and the "flower of wealth and glory."
(Pictured: "Moran" or "Peony" by Jihong Park Bong-soo)

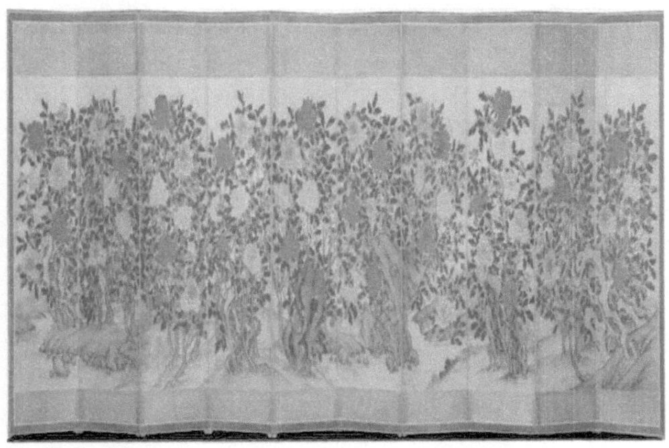

In the royal court of the Joseon Dynasty (1392-1910), the peony flower was commonly featured on folding screens that were used in various ceremonies, such as ; including ancestral rituals, royal weddings, and rituals in the Royal Ancestral Shrine.

The Three Peony Flowers

Emperor Taizong of China
Once sent the Queen Shin of Silla
A painting of three flowers of peony
In red, purple and white chromaticity.

With its actual seeds, he sent along
That when the queen planted it in her garden among
Other flowers, she knew even though the flower was pretty
It probably does not have much fragrant actually.

Her words were then proven to be accurate
When the flowers bloomed, wilted and decayed
Without giving off any scent at all, she said
As people were surprised that she had known of it ahead.

The painting showed no butterfly or bee beside the flowers

Which made her surmise outright the outcome ever

And when the Emperor sent her the gift he was certainly

Mocking the Queen for not having a husband or family.

The peony represented elegance and solemnity

And was nicknamed the "monarch of flowers" and prosperity

They have large, much divided leaves that are glossy

Borne on annual stems produced by rootstocks and fleshy.

The peony flower does not have any scent or odor

Which is why butterflies were not interested or held any ardour

Implying the reason why she did not have a spouse nor consort

It was probably because no man was interested to court.

Not being married was seen as something as a negative way

For one's character and status during those days

It was said that, the Fragrance of the Royal Temple

Was built as a response to the mockery of it all.

Peonies, since then, has been identified with her queendom
Since they are equated with her insight and wisdom
It has also been known as the "king of flowers"
And in Chinese culture became the favourite flower.

In late spring and the early summer
Peonies produce large single and double flowers
Of white, pink, rose, and crimson colour deeper
Such endearing beauty to the eyes of the beholder.

Symbolic of love, honor, wealth, romance, and beauty
The peony is given on special occasions traditionally
As an expression of goodwill, joy and prosperity
Because of Queen Shin in the Tang Dynasty.

"Faith gives hope, even in the worst situation or circumstance. When one is in his worst circumstance, or the littlest confidence that one has cannot overpower or subdue the situation, it is only faith and faith alone that can fuel one`s aspiration."

Dream Encounter

A man named Jigwi, who lived near the border
of Goguryeo

Went to Seorabeol and saw the queen passing by and
immediately so

He fell in love with her despite their difference in age
and social status

And was told to do nothing but call out the queen's
name, losing his intelligence obtuse.

Queen Seondeok went to visit a Buddhist temple to
pray

As she was passing by, Jigwi appeared calling out the
queen's name one day

The queen's guard thrust him aside, causing a
commotion

And she was told by her attendants of the man`s
condition.

She was told of his story and took pity on him
inevitably

And allowed him to follow her retinue to the temple unexpectedly

While the queen was praying inside the temple

Jigwi had to wait outside in the pagoda where he fell asleep.

When the queen finally emerged, she noticed Jigwi behind the pagoda temple

She asked her attendants not to disturb the sleeping man inside the hall

But placed her bracelet on Jigwi's chest as a keepsake

That he will surely see as soon as he turns awake.

When Jigwi woke up and saw the bracelet that she had left for him

He was so overwhelmed with joy and love for the queen it seem

That it was then that it was said his whole body turned into a fire

The fierce flames of his love burned down himself in desire.

According to a legend in the story, Jigwi was beaten by the palace guards actually

For calling out the queen's name every day until he could no longer move physically

His soul became a fire spirit and burned down people`s houses and the pagoda

Who were scared of Jigwi's wrath so she made a talisman to block away his pneuma.

In a modern version of the story. Jigwi fell in love with the Queen

Whom he met every night through her restless dream

In her dream, he appeared as a handsome Hwarang Knight

Who gave her predictions and solutions for the crises she faced in her might.

Through Jigwi's assistance, Queen Seon overcame one obstacle after another

They met each other in a bridge in her dream through romantic encounter

But suddenly Jigwi stopped appearing in her mysterious slumber

And the queen started to miss him and began to hopelessly wonder.

But Jigwi was nowhere to be found, and instead

The Queen saw a sleeping beggar near the pagoda`s
stead

When Jigwi woke up, he was overwhelmed with
longing for the queen

He longed to see her face and the sweet memory of
what could have been.

The legend told his heart turned into a fire that spread
through his whole body

Then the fire flew to heaven and the rain started to
fall torrentously

Which ended the long drought and dry-spell
throughout in Silla

Somewhere in the history of Korean Peninsula.

"In every single dream, there is hope. When there is hope, there is a flicker of inspiration. It is in a simple inspiration a staggering reality springs. It is when inspiration springs that every thing implausible becomes possible and this makes all the difference. Never give up with your dreams, no matter how young or old you may be. For the ability to dream and aspire to what your heart desire is what makes your life a little more beautiful and worth waiting for".

The Tale Of Jade Gate

Near the banks of the Seongjin river in the capital city

There was a temple called Yeongmyosametropoli.

In the temple grounds was a pond named Jade Gate where

At the pond on a certain day in winter.

Frogs used to assemble and gather

At the pond and began to croak loudly together.

When this strange phenomenon was reported to the queen

She immediately ordered two of her generals in the scene.

To lead her best soldiers to the western suburb of the city

And to look for the place Cradle of Life valley.

She added that an enemy force would be found there in waiting

Which they would be sure to take by surprise and astonishing.

The two generals led their armies to the valley the queen had mentioned

Near Mt. Bu, and destroyed not only the detachment of 500 Baekje warriors.

They found there, but also a force of 1,200 reinforcements in force

Which came later to aid them in the battleforce.

When asked how she had foreseen the Baekje invasion

Simply because of the croaking of frogs, she continued on.

The queen explained, "A group of angry frogs signifies an army

Jade Gate is an expression for a woman's chastity."

Woman is one of the meanings of Yin and its forces

Which also has the meaning of white, and the white color stands for the West.

So I knew that an army was lying in the West direction

As we say, a man is supposed in some sense to die during the act of creating new creation.

Since the Baekje army was hiding in the valley known as the Cradle of Life

I knew that it would be easy to defeat them in this strife.

This shows that the queen was well-versed in Yin and Yang philosophy

And interpreted all the icons, its balance and order, correctly.

The fact that the queen dealt with the topic openly

In front of her male courtiers also showed her bold audacity.

The Jade Gate

"Life is a gateway of opportunities for optimistic souls and spirits. Those who have faith and those who believe can always look forward for a possible realization of a dream. Hope and enthusiasm in someone`s heart can work miracles and become a channel to an assured portent of reaching one`s aspiration."

The Last Wish

Several days before Queen Seondeok died
She gathered her officials and gave the order to abide.

That when she die, to bury her near the Heaven of
Grieved Merits
Which in Buddhism refers to a certain level of
Heavenly dais.

When asked where the Doricheon was situated in a
direction
She replied that it was on the southern side of Mt.
Namsan Mountain position.

Decades after her death, the king Munmu of Silla
Built and constructed the Sacheonwang-sa .

"Temple of the Four Heavenly Kings"in her tomb
was inscripted
Then the nobles realized that was one of the
Buddha's adage.

"Dori-cheon is above the Sacheonwang-cheon", was
accomplished by the queen in this

However, rather than prediction, some historians
think of it as her last wish.

Having suffered so much jealousy and prejudice for
being a woman during her reign

This may be a way to show her desire to be
reincarnated as a man in her next life and domain.

"When one's heart is full of wishes, the probabilities of favorable outcomes is highly at its best. It is because the Fate is somewhere around watching and on its way to knit its thread and spin the tapestry of events in your life. If something is meant to be yours, it will be yours. It may be delayed, deferred, or postponed. Still, it will never be too late. What's bound to happen, will happen. Some may block your way, some may put hurdles on your steps, some may even push you and throw you to the dumps. Whatever way, you will surely reach your destination since this is the path best designed for you to trod and explore."

Taejo Of Joseon

Taejo of Joseon born Yi Seong-gye, was the founder and first ruler of the Joseon dynasty of Korea. After ascending to the throne, he changed his name to Yi Dan and reigned from 1392 to 1398.

Born in 1367 as the fifth son of King Taejo and Queen Sinui, he was qualified as an official of the Goryeo dynasty in 1382. During his early days, he helped his father in earning the support of the citizens and of many influential figures in the government. Yi Bang-won helped his father in the founding of the new dynasty by assassinating powerful officials such as JeongMong-ju, who remained loyal to Goryeo.

He was called Prince Jeongan during the reign of King Taejo and was taught by Confucian scholars.

Yi-Seong-Gye "King Taejo" of Joseon (r. 1392-1408)
Founder of Korea's Joseon Dynasty

Rule Of Taejong

Taejong of Joseon, also named Yi bang Won

Third ruler of Korea`s Dynasty Joseon

Born on June year thirteen sixty seven

Helped his father to extend his support with their
citizens.

Son of King Taejo, fifth in the order of birth among
his siblings

He founded a new dynasty, together with his father
King

They overthrowedGoryeo to establish a new dynasty
Joseon

By assassinating powerful officials who remained loyal
to Goryeo.

However, the King favouredTaejong`s brother to be
crown prince later on

Together with the Prime Minister, they plotted
Jeonjong to be in position

But in contrast, Bangwon sought direct rule through absolute monarchy

And all their differences contributed to deep political tension ultimately.

Bangwon led a coup d`etat while the King was mourning for his wife

This incident instantly became known as the palace`s First Strife

The King was aghast at the fact that his sons are willing to kill each other

This event also led to the death of two of his sons and their supporters.

The King immediately abdicated and crowned his second son as new ruler

Yi Bang-gwa also called King Jeongjong absolutely put into power

One of Jeongjong`s first act as monarch was to revert the capital to Gaeseong

Where he is believed to have been considerably more comfortable all along.

Yet although in conflict with Bangan, his disgruntled older brother

Bangwon also yeaned and successfully retained his
power

He defeated his brother`s forces and executed him
into exile

Assumed the throne at long last and became the third
King of Joseon awhile.

In the beginning of his reign, his father refused to
relinquish the royal seal

He began to initiate policies he believed would prove
his qualification to will

His first act as a king was to abolish the privilege
enjoyed by the upper echelons

And the aristocracy to maintain private armies and
independent forces on.

His second act was concerning land ownership, he
then revised the legislation

So their national income increased twofold through
recording of state and taxation

He created a strong central government and an
absolute monarchy

He played an influential role in scrapping
the Dopyeong Assembly.

A council of the old government administration that
held a monopoly

In court power during the waning years of the
Goryeo dynasty

He promoted Confucianism, which was more a
political philosophy

He closed many temples, seized their possessions and
added them to the treasury.

He promoted publications, commerce and education

Founded the royal guard, secret police and ruled with
a fist of iron

He remained a controversial figure who killed many
of his rivals

Yet ruled effectively to improve the populace`s lives.

"Serving the public does not only mean one has the power to rule and one know how to exercise power. There is a fervent need for a leader to have a deep sense of righteousness in the order of things and his commitment to serve with a heart. An efficient leader is one who is compassionate and humane, one who understand the sufferings and predicament of his people."

Sejong Of Joseon

Personal name Yi Do widely known as Sejong the Great was the fourth ruler of the Joseon dynasty of Korea. Initially titled Grand Prince Chungnyeong , he was born as the third son of King Taejong and Queen Wongyeong. In 1418, he was designated as heir after his eldest brother, Crown Prince Yi Je, was stripped of his status. Today, King Sejong is regarded as one of the greatest leaders in Korean history.

Born in 1397, Sejong succeeded to the throne at the age of 22 when his father, King T'aejong, abdicated in his favor. Chosen in place of his oldest brother, the rightful heir to the throne, whose lifestyle and conduct were deemed unfit for a king, Sejong became the fourth monarch of the Choson Kingdom.

King Sejong the Great
Most Respected King in Korean History

Reign Of Sejong

Sejong the Great was the fourth ruler of the Joseon Dynasty

The third son of King Taejong, was designated Crown Prince respectively.

He ascended to the throne during the first four years of his reign absolutely

Sejong reinforced Korean Confucian and Neo-Confucian policy.

He enacted major legal amendments and personally

Created and promulgated Hangul, the Korean alphabet traditionally.

He also encouraged advancements of science and technology

Introduced them to stimulate economic growth measures and strategy.

He dispatched military campaigns to the north part of
the territory and location

Instituted the Samin policy to attract new settlers to
the region.

To the south, he helped subjugate Japanese pirates
during the Ōei Invasion

He is regarded as one of the greatest kings in the
history of Korea`s Joseon.

After his father's death, he governed as the sole
monarch

And though he became increasingly ill, he still left a
mark.

The appellation "the Great" was given posthumously

To almost every ruler of Goryeo and Joseon
respectively.

Yet this title is usually associated
with Gwanggaeto and Sejong

When he reached twelve, he became Grand Prince
Chungnyeong.

Sejong's ascension to the throne was unique as certainly

Even in retirement he continued to influence government policy.

While making Hangul, shortly before his death, Sejong slowly lost his sight

However, King Sejong continued to study and create Hangul with his might.

King Sejong reorganized the Korean government by appointing in position

People from different social classes as civil servants in occupation.

He performed official government events according to Confucianism

He encouraged people to behave according to the teachings of him.

As a result, Confucianism became the social norm of their society

Drastically reducing the power and wealth of the Buddhist hierarchy.

Buddhist monks wielded strong influence in politics
and the economy

With the dominant powers of the Joseon dynasty.

Now being devout Confucianists who viewed
Buddhism as a false philosophy

Officials accused the temples and monks of being
corrupted by power and money.

This strengthened the opposition to Buddhism within
the Joseon government

Where temple lands were seized and redistributed for
development.

Sejong`s reform of land system was factor to the
suppression of Buddhism however

Buddhist temples and monks lost large amounts of
economic influence and power.

Sejong also ordered a decree against the Korean
Muslim community

That had held special status and stipends since
the Yuan dynasty.

In the early years of the Joseon Dynasty Korea's
economy was based on

The most common forms of currency with a barter
system with grain and cotton.

Under Sejong`s rule the government attempted to
develop a national currency

Modeled off on the Chinese Kaiyuan Tongbao
overtly.

It was a bronze coin backed by a silver standard equal
to 600 grams of silver

But they ceased as they were expensive to produce
with the exchange rate rather.

Yi Hyang was the longest holder of the position
of Crown Prince

Holding the position in a record of twenty nine years.

When he was an eight-year-old Yi Hyang was
educated by ministers

Until his own accession to the throne, he served as
regent.

Yi Hyang ascended the Joseon throne as King Munjong

His reign marked the beginning of an imbalance of power at court strong.

Kim Bi-hwan describes the "interaction of the royal authority and pillars

Administrative, remonstrative power, and collective authority of scholars".

"There is a substantial difference between serving people and governing people. The former can teach a leader humility, humanity and compassion. The latter might misguide a leader to complacency, arrogance and conceit. That is why it takes a strong personality for a leader to control power rather than power to control his character."

Queen Yun

She was an 11th generation descendant of General Yun Gwan, later known as the Deposed Queen Lady Yun, served Prince Yeonsan's father, Seongjong, as a concubine until the death of Queen Gonghye, Seongjong's first wife. With no royal heir, the King was urged by counselors to take a second wife to secure the royal succession. Lady Yun was chosen for her beauty, and was formally married in 1476.

The Tragedy Of Yoon And Hyeol

Queen consort of Joseon

Also known as Yoon and Jeheon

Consort to King Yi Hyeol to secure the royal succession

Until fourteen seventy nine in her deposition.

Lady Yoon was chosen for her beauty

In marrying the most powerful man of the country

Temperamental and jealous though she may be

Does that make her a villain or a victim having a child
so early?

The King at a young age of fifteen summers
And she at only about barely a year older
Were fated to be binded together
Their youthful lives intertwined forever.

In her childish temperamental streak one evening
It was said that she strucked the King
The Grand Queen Insu, upon discovering this
information
Ordered her into exile and later executed her by
poison.

That was the sad tale of youthful Yoon and Hyeol
Such pity their love story was misunderstood by all
No one ever attempted to consider the fact and know
How it was to be saddled with duty before you even
grow.

"Some old traditions, customs and mores are still being practiced in modern times. In these days of current technology, some people still believe in applying primordial measures since old practices almost always turns out right for their predecessors. However, there are times when a more telematic approach needs to be observed. Whatever process one follows, accurate solution seems more appropriate in a given situation or predicament."

Crown Prince Hyomyeong

Born Yi Yeong, and posthumously honored as King Munjo, was a member of the Joseon Dynasty.The prince was the eldest son of King Sunjo, husband of Queen Sinjeong and father of King Heonjong. In 1817, the prince was admitted to the Sungkyunkwan. In 1819, he was titled Crown Prince of Joseon. A genius in literature and the arts, he created several court dances) and used court ritual and the arts to validate and augment the King's control over the government.

Hyomyeong first became active in politics when he was only 18, due to his father being ill. Known to have pursued various political reforms, the prince served as Regent in 1827 until his death 3 years later at age 20. He did have some enemies amongst his maternal relatives, but avoided nepotism and was a talented writer, composer and choreographer.

Love In The Moonlight

(Jan eun da Jassnabwayo)

Prologue

I.

This is a story from Joseon Dynasty

Foretold and retold many times in history

It happened somewhere in Korea's 19th century

Of Hong sam-non and Prince Hyomyeong love story.

II.

Both disguised as Hong Ra On and Lee Yeong secretly

Two hiding shadows crossed each other`s path in destiny

Each has its own reason for doing their masquerade

They may be of pure intention, still, both played victims of this charade.

Love In The Moonlight

(Jan eun da Jassnabwayo)

Hong sam-non (Disguised as Ra On)

III.

In the backdrop of a field of beautiful flowers, we met

The field abundant with crepe myrtle trees, how can I forget

In Damyang Garden I saw you wearing a gray Hanbok dress

I thought a butterfly fluttered in my stomach and chest.

IV.

At the first sight of you, you just took me by surprise

You must be a warrior, that I instantly surmised

You are the moonlight drawn by clouds, I knew

The excitement to see you once more lingered and grew.

V.

Here I am again filled with sad melancholy

Wishing to catch a sight of you in my silent reverie

Here in this flower garden, sitting alone in a swing

In Gwanghalluwon Garden, precious memory it brings.

VI.

My heart you have snatched and easily conquered

My precious warrior, you fill me with emotions I have
not yet mastered

Like the moonlight covered by clouds

You had me hanging suspended in doubts.

VII.

My moonlight dream, if you really are my guide

If your light can truly show me far and wide

Why my thoughts travel along the dark crevices of
illusion

And search the moonlight concealed by clouds,
hiding alone.

VIII.

What magic do you possess, perchance, tell me
What kind of spell did you cast on me
Why do I keep thinking of the places where we met
Like seeing you in the Naganeupsong Village upon
sunset.

IX.

The lantern festival in the folk village at dark

The glimpses I see of you in Seodongyo theme park

Seeing you once more in Geonggi Shrine bamboo
forest

Why do I keep bumping at you at those instances?

X.

You are my jagiya, my handsome love in the
moonlight

My sonata, my haesarang, my tender delight

My ever gentle yeobo, my wangjunim, my other half

I am destined to be your shadow who constantly
follows you, my guph.

XI.

The courtyard in Hauseong Palace etched in my
memory

The dancing concubines in Jeonju school reminds in
subtlety

In Champandaek House, when I fell into your arms

The sweet sudden kiss in the Garden of Morning
Calm.

박보검
김유정
구르미 그린 달빛
박보검
김유정

XII.

The lovely little pond where we both stood close together

The colorful lantern-filled night sky where lights flew higher and higher

Seems to be urging me to uncover this secrecy

Hidden no more, I must reveal my identity.

XIII.

I cannot deny how instantly you got me impress

Seeing you now in that Mandarin Hanbok of dark blue dress

The sangtugwan ring in your hat, your belt designed in four toes dragon

Symbolizing you as the Crown Prince, there's no denying your position.

XIV.

While your jade green colored robe with inner lilac garments fit you well

That beaded blue and red strings hanging off your hat highly shows and tell

You're every inch the perfect royalty, now I do take note of this

Why did I ever think otherwise, that was such a foolish miss.

XV.

For you are my beamlight, my moonbow, my fantasy up above

You are my dream come true, my haekkeo, my only love

You are my eternal guide, I am your shadow who always follow you around

You are such a delight upon my sight, my shining "Moonlight Drawn By Clouds".

Moonlight Drawn By Clouds

(Gureumi Geurin Dalbit)

XVI.

You pretended to be a dashing Eunuch and servant
I was carried away by that debonair stunt
Why, I thought, am I falling for a man helplessly
What a shame, to be this confused desperately.

XVII.

The greyish silvery moon in its naughty crescent shine hid its face

What are you concealing ever fascinating moon, must I trace?

Do not hide to me your ever beauteous fancy secret

I ask you not to deceive me and fill me with regret.

XVIII.

The Crown Prince, the man every girl wants to win
The carefree me, Lee Yeong, Crown Regent at
seventeen
Fell I to someone not of my own league and status
Like a moonlight veiled by cloud cumulus.

XIX.

I am supposed to be the one who should be
pretending

Masquerade myself as a warrior for my sister's
pleading

In her quest to find her true love waiting

Destiny played a trick on my own life's doing.

XX.

Who are you that you easily caught my fancy
A little Eunuch, plain and nothing extra ordinary
How can such a young boy just like a man like me
Be interesting in a way, makes me wonder so
infuriatingly.

XXI.

What could be your secret that made me doubt my
own person

You are such the shrouded cloud to this moonlight's
confusion

I couldn't put the missing pieces of the puzzle that
you are

My heart tells me you're a different person from what
I see from afar.

XXII.

If I had known at first your true identity

I wouldn't be in torment with doubts and uncertainty

Hong sam-non, that is the true woman you are

Lovely as the moon and beautiful as the star.

XXIII.

Seeing you in a different way, wearing that ballerina
dress

Your flimsy dancing costume, your carefree flowing
tress

That total transformation from Eunuch dress code of
torquoise and blue

Disguised as a court lady, I clearly saw that my
intuition was true.

XXIV.

I am your shining moon, you are my pretty little cloud
bit

Nae guleum, my constant shadow, my sweet

The reason why there seems to be some familiarity

Some kind of instant recognition between you and
me.

XXV.

I am Hyomyeong, your wangjanim twin flame
Destined to be the moonlight etched in your name
You are the cloud who enveloped this moon's vision
The veil who concealed my sight and masked in
pretention.

XXVI.

I thought I lost you in my search, eternity seemed to pass me by

But I found you my forever, my puffy silky cloud in the sky

I am the moonlight wrapped in your grey white tiny feathery strings

Floating in your embrace, flying higher in your wings.

XXVII.

My love in the moonlight, seeing you this close and near to me at last

I wondered if I have met you somewhere in my distant past

You are my "Dance of a Spring Nightingale", my sole inspiration

Saranghaeyo, kamsahamnida, I whisper to you with tender devotion.

"Love and Moonlight. Two enchanting elements in providing an ambiance of a romantic rendezvous. The scenic view, the flower garden, and the significance the moonlight, all the more invokes the subtle mood and the perfect moment that will hold a lifetime of memories. The magic of two shadows in the silhouette of darkness, illuminated by the glinty, silvery moon, bringing the music of a cascading heartbeat and rhythm of love. Where the moon becomes Cupid, and its light becomes Psyche personified. Where love is in the moonlight, and the moonlight is drawn by clouds. "

Epilogue (Narrator)

XXVIII.

The character of this was based in the real life of Hyomyeon

Korea's Crown Prince of Dynasty Joseon

Somewhere far in that distant land in eighteen o nine he was born

Who in his lifetime pursued various political reforms.

XXIX.

He was considered a genius in literature and the art

Through his artistic sense has captured many hearts

A dancer himself, he created several court dances
beautifully

Including one considered as the most important in
Korean court ritual history.

XXX.

Served as Regent in eighteen twenty seven until his
death in eighteen thirty

At a young and budding of age of only twenty

The moonlight drawn by cloud as the title suggest

Leaves us love's legacy as one of Korea's best.

"The love of one's ruler to his subjects and his country reflects in his character through implementation of his rules and policies. His mandate is for his people, and his commitment is upon his service. If he abides upon the rules of the land for the benefit and goodness of his people, it is in his heart to serve. But if he only serve to the merit of those in a position and for the benefit of himself, then public service is not for him. The world in general truly needs a servant with a heart for service of humanity."

Princess Seonhwa

She was the daughter of King Jinpyeong of Silla and wife of King Mu of Baekje. As such, she was Queen consort of Baekje from 600 CE to an unknown year. Seonhwa's existence is controversial due to the discovery of evidence that points to King Uija's mother as being Queen Sataek, and not Seonhwa as indicated by historical records.

According to the Legend chapter of SamgukYusa, she was the third daughter of King Jinpyeong of Silla and his wife Queen Maya of Silla and was famous for her beauty. Seonhwa's sisters were Princess Deokman (later Queen Seondeok of Silla) and Princess Cheonmyeong.

The Ballad Of Sudong

The protagonist of the story Su Dong according to
SamgukYusa

In Korea`s oldest folk songs and its first hyangga

Was a commoner from Technology Institute
Taehaksa

Spied by other countries like Koguryo and Silla.

The institute was always in danger of espionage and
spying

The roles of monk as industrial snoopers are
deceiving

As advanced guards of intelligence war at that era

One would never guess they stick their noses at
other`s dilemma.

To solve the problems of excessive dryness of their
land

They released earthworms and used ondol or hot
floor

To decrease the humidity of their homes bit further

They used the precipitation of temperature and
weather.

Sudong met and fell with Princess Seonhwa

Daughter of the King of their rival Silla

While his rival BuyeoSeon plotted against him

He wrote the Ballad of Sudong, a lyrical rhythm.

Hearing that Princess Sonhwa was beautiful and
enchanting

He wrote a song about the princess telling

About the story of her visiting his room every night

The King whereupon hearing this was suddenly
grasped by fright.

So spreads the song The Ballad of Sudong

When King Chinpyong her father hears the song

He condemns the princess Seonhwa to exile

And detained herin the Palace Dungeon awhile.

Sodong picks her up and took her to Paekche

And they became the Royal couple of the country
Baekje

Sudong became King Mu much later

The 30th King of Paekche Dynasty thereafter.

"When one ruler takes his duties to heart, half of his life remains dedicated for the service alone. The other half comprises the other fifty percent. Duty to his religion, to his family, to his friends and to himself takes a backseat. For the most important and pressing work to do is his duty upon his oath of office. No one or nothing else must rise above this so called pact for his country. Deliverance of good service must always be at the helm in order for a nation to rise and achieve its purpose."

Cheoljong

He was the 25th king of the Joseon Dynasty. He was a second cousin once removed to the heirless Heonjong of Joseon, as well as a great-great-grandson of Yeongjo of Joseon. He ascended the throne at the age of 19.

He was born as the 3rd and youngest son of Yi Gwang, Prince Jeongye (who died on December 14, 1841), and his 1st concubine, Lady Yeom of the YongdamYeom clan, on Ganghwa Island. His name was originally Yi Won-beom but upon ascending the throne his name was legally changed to Yi Byeon (or Yi Seong).

Portrait of King Cheoljong

Painted in 1861, this is the only surviving royal portrait depicting King Cheoljong's physical appearance, as well as Joseon Era royal military attire; partly damaged during the Second Fire of Yongdusan, Busan during the early hours of 26 December 1954

Cheoljong Of Joseon

Cheoljong of Joseon was the 25th king of Joseon
Dynasty

Probably one of the most famous era of Korean
country

But at the beginning of the nineteenth century

There was corruption and embezzlement from the
treasury.

The Andong Kim clan had seized extreme power

The only aim of their clan was their influence
everywhere

Such that it reached to much staggering proportions

And were taken to extreme levels with inevitable
exploitation.

Accompanied by natural calamities and disasters

Added by one act of rebellion into another

The fierce campaign to dominate the royal house led
to a situation

In which all representatives of their family fled to
escape in notion.

When royal family produced intelligent candidates for the accession

They were either accused with mutiny and with treason

No acceptable candidate can be found to succeed to the throne

As vulnerable as Cheoljong to their control and manipulation.

Cheoljong was selected for adoption

By the senior Dowager Queen Sunwon

He ascended to the throne at the age of nineteen

As the deceased King`s distant relative and kin.

His family has been in exile since the Catholic Persecution

When the envoys arrived in Ganghwa Island, they instantly known

And in the midst of that degradation pertaining to his illiteracy,

They found the remnants of the clan in wretched poverty.

Cheoljong died at the age of 32 by suspected foul play

That was the sad story of his life in such a desperate way

Knowledge and recognition is a sure path to stay in power

No use to rule if you are in a string as an overshadowed follower.

"No ruler will stay in power if he allows weakness and ignorance to get the better of him. Aside from a strong personality, a ruler must have character and firm disposition. He must know when to listen and when to hear, when to move forward and when to take a backseat. Power is not a position, rather, it is the position that put him into power. Relatively, he must understand that time somehow is such a fleeting matter, and the inconstancy of his fate is determined not by whatever surrounds him in the present, but by a more definitive factor called time."

The Andongs

Cheoljong who was the 25th king of the Joseon Dynasty

Ascended the throne at the age of nineteen youthfully

He was born as the 3rd and youngest son of Yi Gwang Yi

Upon ascending the throne, he was legally changed to Yi Seong instantly.

The Andong Kim clan, who provided the state with several Queens

Managed to seize power almost everywhere in Joseon years

This resulted to a breeding ground for unrest and social stagnation

Since the Andongs only claim was their influence`s preservation.

Corruption and embezzlement from the treasury and its inevitable exploitation

Were taken to extreme levels and reached staggering proportions

One rebellion after another was accompanied by
natural disasters and debacle

In which almost all members of the Royal Family fled
from the capital.

Their fierce campaign to dominate the Royal House
had led to a situation

When the Royal Family produced intelligent and
appropriate candidates for the accession

They were either executed, sent into exile or accused
of treason

When Heonjong died, there was no acceptable
candidate to succeed to the throne.

Cheoljong ascended to the throne at the age of
nineteen

After King Heonjong died without a heir or any kin

As a distant relative of the deceased King, Cheoljong
was selected for adoption

And allowed him to ascend to the throne by Queen
Dowager Sunwon.

The future Cheoljong was found on Ganghwa Island

Where his family had been in exile since the Catholic
Persecution

When the envoys arrived on Ganghwa Island

They found the exiled remnants of the Royal Clan.

Barely surviving in wretched poverty, and in the midst
of that degradation

19-year old Yi Won-beom was proclaimed King
though from the start of Joseon

The Kings had given top priority to the education of
their sons

Cheoljong couldn`t even read a single word on the
notice delivering congratulations.

For the Andong Kims, Cheoljong was an excellent
choice and option

His illiteracy made him vulnerable to their controlling
actions

And though he ruled the country for 13 years, until
his very last days

It was said he had not learned how to move in royal
ways.

As part of the Andong Kim's manipulation of
Cheoljong

The clan married Cheoljong to Kim Mun-geun's
daughter, known as Queen Cheorin

Cheoljong died at the age of 32 by suspected foul play
of the Andong Kim clan,

The same clan which made him King, without any
surviving male descendant.

Cheoljong was responsible for some very important
rectifications

Noble reforms on paper but apparently not followed
religiously on

Universal corruption originates too high up for it to
be rooted

This Machiavellian play was fairly dangerous ahead.

There was also a degree of international uncertainty

The French and English victory over the Chinese in
late 1860

Heavy taxes added to all their people`s misery

And the young king seemed more intent on perpetual
debauchery.

Alcohol, food and women occupied his days and his
reign lasted for as long as it did

He was weak and did not interfere in the plans of
those who surrounded him indeed

In the fall of 1963, it became apparent that the King`s
days are numbered

He was extremely swollen and barely able to move by
the putrid hand of life`s end.

Another member of the royal family, Yi Ha-jon

Decided to take matters into his own hands and seize
the throne

His coup failed in its infancy and with his life, he paid
for his transgression

Rather than executed, he was allowed to end his life
in a more dignified manner with poison.

In December a comet ominously appeared in the
night skies,

The superstitious consulted ancient tomes of
prophecy lies

The signs were all there,the king was dying

The dynasty and the kingdom is failing.

With Cheoljong's death, the Joseon dynasty

Moved even closer to the precipice of collapse and
uncertainty

The Joseon-Machiavellian Heungseon Daewongun
acted as regent, long

Until his 12 year old son came of age and was known
as King Gojong.

"History teaches us the best lessons education and academics cannot provide. Experiences and examples best show us how to deal with situations first hand. There is no definite formula or equation when it comes to life`s certain decisions. But stories and occurrences from the past best supplies us how to face certain circumstances. Experience is still the best indicator on what, how and why we are presented with certain situations as we try and able to deal of them."

Queen Cheorin

Queen Cheorin, also known as Queen Dowager Myeongsun was Queen consort of Joseon by marriage to King Cheoljong. Lady Kim was born into the (new) Andong Kim clan. As part of the Andong Kim clan's manipulation of King Cheoljong, she married him on November 17, 1851. The Queen eventually gave birth to a son, Yi Yung-jun, in 1858, but he died less than a year later, in 1859.

On January 16, 1864, King Cheoljong died without a male heir. This was suspected to be the result of foul play by the Andong Kim clan, which had risen to power through intermarriage with the House of Yi. Queen Cheorin died on June 12, 1878, and is buried in Inreung, Seoul, with her husband.

Queen Consort Cheorin

Queen Cheorin also known as Queen consort of Joseon.

Also called as Queen Dowager Myeongsun, married to King Cheoljon

Born into the Andong Kim clan as the eldest daughter of Kim Mun-geun

And his second wife, Lady Heungyang of the clan Min Yeoheung.

As part of the Andong Kim clan's manipulation of King Cheoljong,

There was a suspected result of foul play by the clan Kim Andong

He fell deeper under his illness as result of this manipulation

Until he died without any male heir to for his succession.

The selection of the next King was in the hands of three dowagers:

Queen Shinjeong, who is Prince Hyomyeon`s mother

Queen Hyohyeon and Queen Cheorin, that was a scrupulous plan

Why the Queen Dowager saw an opportunity to advance the cause of Pungyan Jo clan.

Yi Ha-eung's family branch belonged to an obscure line of descent of the Jeonju Yi clan relation

Which survived the political intrigue that frequently embroiled the Joseon court by forming no affiliations

Yi Ha-eung himself was ineligible for the throne due to a law, that any heir had to be part of the generation

After the most recent incumbent of the throne, his son Yi Myeong-bok was a possible successor and elation.

The Pungyang Jo clan saw that Yi Myeong-bok was only twelve years old then

And would not be able to rule in his own name until he came of age when

They could easily influence Yi Ha-eung, who would be acting as Regent for the future King

As soon as news of Cheoljong's death reached Yi Ha-eung through his intricate network of spies and quisling.

He and the Pungyang Jo clan took the royal seal which was considered necessary

For a legitimate reign and aristocratic recognition which can effectively

Give Queen Sinjeong absolute power to select the successor to the throne

By the time Cheoljong's death had become a known fact, the Andong Kim clan was powerless and alone.

Yi Myeong-bok was appointed Prince Ikseong by Grand Queen Dowager Sinjeong

While practicing her regency, the Queen invited the Daewongun to assist his young son Gojong

The Queen may have renounced her right and though she kept the title, the Daewongun was in fact the true ruler

Until the time Queen Cheorin died and is buried in Inreung with her husband thereafter.

"Everyone must be equal. No race, colour, occupation or national identity must be above the rest. The need for respect and compassion is too apparent and must be taught along with our society's quest for education. Goodness of character and disposition will never go out of style. No matter how advance our knowledge becomes, we must not forget such basic courtesy as that of being human."

The Legend Of Three Kingdoms

The name "Korea" was derived from the name Goryeo

A Korean Kingdom founded in 918 also called Koryo

First used in the early 5th century the Goguryeo

Which achieved the true national unification of their Kingdom`s Trio.

The once prosperous kingdom of Later Silla

Which had ruled much of the Korean Peninsula

Began crumbling by the late 9th century

When Baekje was conquered by the military.

Unified Silla was initially a period of peace

Without a single invasion for a span of two hundred years

As it engaged in international trade from as distant as the Middle East

With the descendants of the Baekje and Goguryeo refugees.

"Desire for power can change a person's attitude. In his quest for power, he can only become two things: good or bad. Upon his seat in power, it is a real test of his character. And only time will determine how effectively his true person emerged through apparent manifestation of his deeds."

Empress Ki/Empress Gi

Also known as Empress Qi (Chinese) or ÖljeiKhutuk (Mongolian) was one of the primary empresses of Toghon Temur of the Yuan dynasty and the mother of Biligtü Khan, who would become an emperor of Northern Yuan. She was originally from an aristocratic family of the Goryeo dynasty and served as Imperial Concubine of ToghonTemür. She became a Grand Empress, during the last years of the Yuan dynasty, she became one of the most powerful woman, controlling the Yuan dynasty economically and politically.

Empress Ki was born in Haengju modern Goyang, Goryeo to a lower-ranked aristocratic family of bureaucrats. Her father was Gi Ja-oh. In 1333, the teenage Lady Gi was among the concubines sent to Yuan by the Goryeo kings, who had to provide a certain number of beautiful teenage girls to serve as concubines of the Mongol Emperors once every three years. It was considered prestigious to marry Goryeo women. Extremely beautiful and skilled at dancing, conversation, singing, poetry, and calligraphy, Lady Gi quickly became the favorite concubine of Toghon Temür. The Emperor Toghon Temür fell in love with her.

The Rise Of Ki

Empress Ki`s history was written in the Ming dynasty

A dynasty that succeeded Yuan tremendously

She was born in Goryeo also known as Koryo

She was the daughter of a lower-level official named
Ki Ja-Ho.

She was sent as a female tribute to the Mongolian
capital of Daidu

And eventually rose to rank at first as a palace servant
when she was new

The Ming dynasty blamed Empress Ki for the
downfall of the Mongolians

Because, they say, of her corruption and extravagance.

She was assigned to be responsible to the Emperor`s
tea

Which gave her access to Emperor Temur`s
sovereignty

She was extremely beautiful and with artistic talents of
many

Toghon Temur was attracted to her immediately.

They shared a love of painting, poetry and astonomy
Until Ki was officially named concubine in thirteen thirty three
Which incurred the wrath of Empress Tanashiri
Which made Ki the targets of her jealousness and cruelty.

It was recorded in history that on one occasion
Tanashiri tortured Ki with a brander white-hot iron
But as a result the history books recorded and recall
Political intrigue at court began to cause Tanashiri`s downfall.

When Ki was made a concubine, two years after
A minister Bayan began to achieve considerable power
He removed from the seat Tanashiri`s father
And purged her relatives and siblings thereafter.

Tanashiri was confined under house arrest later on
And was eventually executed by venomous poison
With the position of empress becoming vacant

Temur planned to install Lady Ki fast as he want.

But Bayan persuaded the emperor to marry a Mongol

A girl from Khongirad tribe, from descendants of
ancient Wuku all

The said Empress was Bayan Khutugh, his niece

Depicted as a retiring woman who did not resent Ki
at least.

In 1340, Empress Bayan fell out of power and place

Although she retained her title, she was sent away
from the palace

One month after Empress Bayan's downfall

As Second Imperial Consort, Ki was promoted and
installed.

Thus, Lady Ki reigned as empress in all but name

Yet all she wasn't able to attain in position, she gained
in fame.

As the unofficial empress, Ki created a special
government agency

Wherein she wielded a wide-ranging authority.

Ki was actively involved in many philanthropic works
widely

And continued to sponsor Buddhism tremendously

She was also responsible for promoting Korean
culture in China

Proof of her shrewd sharp mind and intellectual
formula.

Her tax collection so secured Empress Ki's finances

As she eventually gained income through her various
investments.

To consolidate her power in the palace,

Lady Ki gained many supporters at last.

She gave many Korean-born eunuchs positions

Within her special government agency delegations.

One of whom was Park Bul-hwa, who was her closest
servant

Who has been a loyal and trustworthy personal
assistant.

Though she did not have a favourable reputation in
her home country

Joseon dynasty portrayed her having ambitious and
pleasure seeking family

It was said she betrayed her country by invading her
homeland, however,

Her family prospered from her position and often abused their power.

Ki became the monarch of China unofficially

Learning how to rule by reading Woman`s Book of Filial Piety

While the emperor began to lose interest in state affairs gradually

And gave the whole power to run the State to his beloved Ki.

What happened afterwards is like a blank page in history

Because The History of The Yuan ended with the flight of imperial family

Toghon Temur died on May thirteen seventy of dysentery

So Ayushiridara was proclaimed ruler of the Great Yuan dynasty.

It is unclear if Empress Ki ever became the empress dowager.

Although we do not know much about her life later

What is clear is that she was a strong and powerful leader

She was a remarkable woman that Korea will always remember.

Regardless of whether Empress Ki deserves her negative reputation

It is clear that she made a massive impact on Chinese nation

A woman of substance, of intelligence, of courage, of disposition

A woman who left a mark that will never fade as history unfolds on.

"Once in a blue moon, an extra ordinary woman is born. It`s not every day this world gives us someone of her stature, the kind of woman who can make a change. The sort of a woman who can change a woman`s history. This has to be her destiny."

Simply Gi

She is Nyang Nyang
Fierce, fearless fighter
From Koryo
With her boyish stance,
She is a combatant,
A warrior
Who can target you
With her bow and arrow.

She is Lady Gi
Feisty, spunky, gritty
With her manful ways
She is a shooter,
A markswoman, a trooper
Endowed with talent and
such beautiful face
Intellectual, artistic, inventive
Possesing eloquent grace.

She is Empress Gi
From Ming Dynasty
Born in Goryeo
Daughter of Ki Ja-Ho
Sent as female tribute
to the Mongolian capital of Daidu
Became a palace maid,
assigned responsible for the Emperor`s tea,
which gave her access to
the sovereign monarch
by becoming into
the love of his life
and being his
concubine and wife.

Two loves of Ki`s life
Wang Yoo
The father of her child
Her first and greatest love
Her admirer
her lover
her defender

her warrior
Ta-Hwan
Her monarch
her emperor
her husband
her way to fame
and power
her little boyish
potentate and sovereign.

Her two beloved children
Whom Gi never had a chance
to show her love in the open.
Ta Hwan`s son Ayu
And Byul, son of Wang Yoo
Her first son
Also called Maha, who lived an unfortunate life
And went through so many lonely strifes
Used by people evil and vicious
Tanashiri and Empress Dowager nefarious.

Gi originated from Korean language which means
arise or rising

It may also mean vigorous, energetic, strong, climbing

Traits that best describes the Empress who is always
and will be a fighter

Throughout her reign a courageous servicewoman
and combatant soldier.

"There comes a one in a million chance when a
ruler's persona is as colourful as the rainbow itself
and her flamboyant character is like an eternal
blossom that never fades. Such is the identity of a
woman ruler, symbolizing the important symbol of
her country and culture, the principles of her people
and her governance in power. Such identity can never
be forgotten."

The End Of Joseon Dynasty

Joseon ruled over a united Korean Peninsula for more than 500 years, through the Japanese Occupation of 1910. The young Joseon Dynasty endured political intrigues including the "Strife of the Princes". In 1401, Joseon Korea became a tributary of Ming China. In 1592 and 1597, the Japanese under Toyotomi Hideyoshi used their samurai army to attack Joseon Korea. Japanese ships captured Pyongyang and Hanseong (Seoul). Joseon was saved by Admiral Yi Sun-sin. Admiral Yi's victory at the Battle of Hansan-do cut the Japanese supply line and forced Hideyoshi's retreat.

Throughout the 19th century, Japan and Qing China vied for power in East Asia. The First Sino-Japanese War (1894–1895) was fought mainly on Korean soil and ended in defeat for the Qing. Japan took control of Korea's land and natural resources through the end of World War II. China's hegemony over Korea ended with its defeat in the First Sino-Japanese War. The Joseon Kingdom was renamed "The Korean Empire," but in fact, it had fallen under Japanese control.

Japan installed its own officials in the executive and judicial branches of the Korean Imperial government, disbanded the Korean military, and gained control of the police and prisons. Soon, Korea became Japanese in name as well as in fact. The Japanese ruled Korea for the next 35 years until the Japanese surrendered to the Allied Forces at the end of World War II.

"After a storm, there is calm. After chaos, there is order. Some may have lost their battles, but all of us must win the war. A nation must stand and emerge as one, from the rubbles of past differences and difficulties."

About the Author

Gigi Balita was born in Tanza Cavite, Philippines. She co-authored around twenty anthology books published by Poetry Planet. She is also a contributor in other international anthology books published on Amazon, Lulu and Bookemon such as "Songs Of Peace", "Kaleidoscope Of Asia", "Seeking Human Kindness", "The Wit and Wisdom Of Thought Leaders", "Illusive Hearts" and "A Thousand Words".

She published her first book "In Love With Ekphrasy" January 2021 under Poetry Planet Publishing House. The book was chosen by prestigious judges of Ybarra Scholars and Fellows as the winner of Best English Poetry Book 2022 in the first Ophir Book Awards in which she was conferred an Honoris Causa, Honorary Doctorate degree in Literature (DLitt) and degree of Fellow of the Order of Writers (FOWr). The said award is ISO 9001:2015 certified and Department of Education accredited through Scholarship, Virtue and Human Excellence Quality DepEd Regional Advisory 032 s. 2021.

www.ingramcontent.com/pod-product-compliance
Lightning Source LLC
Chambersburg PA
CBHW021443150726
47989CB00001B/364